POC

THE
BIBLE

—————— *Edited by* ——————
JOHN O. GOOCH
&
JACK A. KELLER, JR.

ABINGDON PRESS
Nashville

POCKET GUIDE TO THE BIBLE

Library of Congress Cataloging-in-Publication Data

Pocket guide to the Bible / John O. Gooch, Jack A. Keller, Jr.,
    editors.
      p.   cm.
    ISBN 0-687-31680-4 (alk. paper)
    1. Bible—Criticism, interpretation, etc.   I. Gooch, John O.
II. Keller, Jack A.
BS538.P63   1990
220.6'1—dc20   90-21914

MANUFACTURED IN THE UNITED STATES OF AMERICA

EDITORS' PREFACE

When the United Methodist Publishing House announced plans to publish a Cokesbury edition of the New Revised Standard Version of the Bible, the two of us were invited to develop a new set of study helps for readers to be printed with the biblical text. Since some of the standard helps would already be included, we were free to develop additional study helps for lay readers that would be unique to the Cokesbury edition.

On some topics, we felt comfortable writing new pieces ourselves. John wrote the essay "Canonization and Translation." Jack prepared "How to Study a Bible Passage" and co-authored (with George B. Thompson, Jr.) the essay "The Authority of the Bible." On other topics, we depended on the talents of writers and scholars across the church. George B. Thompson, Jr., wrote "The History of the Bible," as well as co-authoring the essay on authority. Jerald H. Jackson developed "The Centrality of Scripture." "The Geography of Palestine" was written by Edward P. Blair. The longest piece, "Major Themes in Scripture," was prepared by Chester A. Pennington. While both of us were involved in shaping the project and identifying contributors, John did the "hands on" editing of all the entries.

We are pleased that Abingdon Press is publishing these helps in this volume of the Pocket Guide Series. We hope this new format will help even more readers begin to unlock the riches of Scripture.

John O. Gooch
Jack A. Keller, Jr.

CONTENTS

THE HISTORY OF THE BIBLE

A Library Takes Shape

The Bible is actually a collection, a library, of many writings. The story of the writing, editing, collecting, and preservation of the Bible is as fascinating as a detective story.

Like a detective story, there are many clues to the Bible's development. Some of these clues may seem tedious and trivial; it is not always easy to see the main direction that is present among the lists of names and all the places and dates. But a general overview is not hard to manage, and it adds immensely to our appreciation of this literature that we claim as Scripture.

Both the Old and New Testaments began as stories circulated by word of mouth. People who lived a nomadic life had little use for written language. Israel's identity grew out of centuries of a wandering existence, with no single place as home and no written records. Storytelling was an art form; and the masters passed on the stories of Abraham and Sarah, Isaac and Rebekah, Jacob and Rachel, Joseph, Moses and Miriam, Joshua, Deborah, and Gideon.

A great surge of writing down old stories seems to have taken place during the times of kings David and Solomon (around 1000 to 922 B.C.). Scholars think that the oral traditions were in danger of being lost when Israel seemed securely based as a nation with political boundaries. David might also have felt that the old stories would give him more backing for his monarchy.

This golden age of Israel's kingdom gave rise to writing about its contemporary experiences as well. First and Second Samuel reveal an insider's view of the royal court during the reigns of Saul and David. Many of the Psalms were probably written during this same period.

The Old Testament

This two-step process—spoken and written— characterizes most of the books of the Old Testament. As time went by, each of the three main sections of the Old Testament came to be accepted as religious standards—they were *canon* (the word *canon* originally meant a measuring reed; the idea here is a standard or authority) for Jewish faith.

Our Story: All of what appears in the Old Testament hinges on the first five books, which form a unit known as the *Torah*. Often referred to as *Law*, Torah is primarily the remembered events of God's people Israel. How this people began, how they survived and came to be a nation—this long, dramatic story is tied to the creation and then sinful fall of the world.

Our Challenge: Centuries after the Exodus and the conquest of the land, Israel faced a series of political crises. During that period of time, the people lost half their kingdom, ten of their tribes, and all their independence. But it was not as though Israel had no choices. At least sixteen persons spoke up through those trying times, calling the leaders and the people to stay true to their God. These *prophets* saw that true spiritual loyalty and justice were the only ways for Israel to maintain its standing. Prophetic writings expose the continual challenge to all peoples who claim trust in God.

Our Reflections: Much of Israel's history was unsettled as the people wandered, fled, fought, and wept over their nation. But during the height of the kingdom of Israel, a number of pieces were composed and recorded. These writings cover such topics as hymns for worship (the Psalms), wisdom (Proverbs), history (Chronicles), and romantic love (Song of Songs). The *Writings* offer both a look at the times and an affirmation of those human elements common to all ages. By A.D. 90, the Jews had closed their canon by recognizing the authority of the Writings—the Psalms, Job, Ecclesiastes, Song of Songs, and the rest.

The New Testament

The Jewish Scriptures were the only scriptures for Jesus and his disciples and for the first generation of the church. Soon, however, Christians began to realize that they had some important needs that were not dealt with in the Jewish Scriptures. Motivated to meet these needs, a number of Christians in the first two generations wrote letters, gospels, and sermons that were circulated among the churches. We can distinguish in the New Testament writings a reflection of the three purposes guiding the New Testament.

1. Getting the Word Out

The earliest Christians, steeped in the Jewish tradition, knew well the power of word of mouth. They also realized that word of mouth was not as effective in the Roman Empire, which increasingly relied on writing. The authority of the spoken word was less accurate and was not as reliable as time passed. Writing, then, preserved the common aspects of the Jesus story.

However, the Christian message was more than a story. This Christian message declared a universal need for all humankind to repent and trust in God through Christ. And why trust in Christ? Because of what Jesus Christ did: his teaching, preaching, and healing; his suffering and death; his resurrection and ascension; and his relationship with future believers. The four Gospels contain most of this material.

2. Fighting Fires

Believe it or not, disagreement among believers took place within the first few years of the Christian movement. Individual preferences and the long-standing differences between Jews and Gentiles created controversies almost immediately. People disagreed about what ideas to believe and what actions were acceptable. The apostle Paul responded to such difficulties by writing letters to various congregations. Perhaps it can be comforting to us to remember that the first Christian writings were spurred by church fights.

3. Guarding the Beliefs

Obviously not everyone who came into contact with this new religious movement agreed with it. Many Jews were not persuaded that Jesus was the long-awaited Messiah. Other persons who became Christians sometimes followed ideas by teachers who interpreted the faith a little too differently. Then there was the Roman government, wary of another movement from such a trouble-making province. These pressures from within and without led New Testament writers to clarify their faith as Christians.

Gospels: One important part of the New Testament consists of stories of Jesus and his influence while on earth and what that influence calls forth from humanity. We have four versions, each offering a distinctive emphasis: Matthew, Mark, Luke, and John. These books are called *gospels* because they tell the *good news* of Jesus Christ.

History of the Early Church: The writer of Luke did not stop at Jesus. He also provided a document describing activities of the first generation of people after Jesus. The Book of Acts covers the period from the day of Pentecost through Paul's mission to the Gentiles and his eventual imprisonment.

Correspondence: Just as family and friends keep in touch today, so the young congregations had contact with one another. Several church leaders wrote to numerous audiences—Paul was the most prolific writer—covering many theological and practical topics.

Finale: As a rousing but mysterious culmination to our Scriptures, the Book of Revelation ends the New Testament. Revelation symbolically explains God's purposes through Christ for the fullness of time and creation.

A New Expanded Canon

What makes this process of canonization so interesting is that no one knows just how it happened. Even though we are aware of some details about the New Testament's development, we still do not know how each Gospel, book, and letter was accepted as having canonical status. We know that certain ideas and views on particular Christian writings were judged by councils to be "heresy," that is, an interpretation that moved too far away from the generally accepted version. But the actual standards of canon and authority are only implied, never stated, in these early decisions.

Old and New

Somehow, believers in the Jewish religious community and the fledgling Christian church trusted in the authority of certain writings. Despite all the stories of hate, murder, war, revenge, and infidelity to God and to fellow human beings, Jews and Christians accepted certain writings as unique and special. Christians added books to the Jewish list. They did so not to oppose, but to continue, what they saw going on in the Hebrew Bible.

Christians believed that Jesus Christ gave an unsurpassable fulfillment to the story of God, which Israel had remembered from Abraham through the rebuilding of the Temple. Jesus was a Jew who referred to Scripture constantly and saw his ministry in its terms (see Matthew 5:17-20). Thus, the Hebrew Bible became the Christian one as well. The writings that we now call the New Testament depend heavily on events and ideas from the Old Testament. Indeed, the New Testament and its proclamation could not exist without the witness of Jewish Scripture. That fact should not surprise us. After all, Christians believed that God whom they knew as the Father of the Lord Jesus Christ was the very same God who called Israel into being.

One distinguished Bible scholar explains the unity of the Bible this way: "The Bible . . . has a unity like that of a great drama. It moves from beginning to end, from creation to new creation. The story deals with people's hopes and fears, their joy and anguish, their ambitions and failures. There is a great deal of diversity in the Bible: different authors, different historical situations, different kinds of theological expression. But underlying all this great variety is the dynamic movement, similar to the plot of a drama, which binds the whole together. The biblical drama, however, is unique in that God appears in the cast. Not only is God the Author who stands behind the scenes prompting and directing the drama but God enters onto the stage of history as the Chief Actor—the protagonist. The biblical plot is the working out of God's purpose for the creation in spite of all efforts to oppose it. The denouement is reached, according to the conviction of the Christian community, when the crucifixion and resurrection of Jesus of Nazareth are proclaimed as the sign of God's decisive victory. In the light of this climactic event the earlier stages of the story are understood with a deeper and larger meaning."[1]

---

[1]From *The Unfolding Drama of the Bible*, by Bernhard W. Anderson (Fortress Press, 1988); pages 14-15.

Adapted from Session 3, "Why Should We Believe the Bible?" of *Foundations: Basics of the Christian Faith for Youth*, Teacher Book (copyright © 1988 by Graded Press); Volume 2, pages 15-17.

THE AUTHORITY OF THE BIBLE

The Breath of God

The most common appeal to the Bible's authority has been by the concept of *inspiration*. For the most part, the Bible does not directly speak about inspiration. One verse, however, is often quoted: "All scripture is inspired by God and is useful for teaching, for reproof, for correction, and for training in righteousness" (2 Timothy 3:16). The word *inspired* in this passage is the Greek *theopneustos*, which literally is *God-winded* or *God-breathed*. It follows a verse referring to "the sacred writings" (verse 15), that is, the Hebrew Bible and possibly some of Paul's letters as well. There is more than one way to speak about inspiration. We can identify four basic ways to think of the inspiration of the Bible.

1. One view holds that every *word* of the Bible is totally inspired by God and contains truth free from error. The assumption here is that God effectively persuaded all biblical writers to put down just the correct words, all the time.

2. Another way to speak of inspiration is to say that it applies to the *ideas* and *concepts* but not to the actual words of the Bible.

15

3. Still other Christians have argued that God inspired not words or ideas but *individual people*. These folks then wrote what they did using the language and thought forms of their culture.

4. Yet another view of inspiration is that God inspired the *community* that produced, preserved, and passed on the writings we call Scripture.

So, inspiration can be defined as all the words, all the ideas, all the writers, or all the believers who kept the writings as Scripture. Each of these positions has its advocates, its strengths, and its critics. Not all Christians agree on how to describe the God-breathed nature of the Bible. But Christians do agree that Scripture is inspired by God. God is the ultimate source or origin of Scripture.

More on the Bible's Authority

Inspiration has not been the only way that Christians have understood God's involvement in the Bible. We can identify three other ways to talk about the authority of Scripture.

1. Probably the most popular of these three takes particular biblical events as the norm for what God is doing and what God is like. God acted in a special way to call Abram, to save Israel from the Egyptians, to preserve the Hebrews through exile, and to save all humanity through Jesus' death and resurrection. This *salvation history* is one basis of the Bible's

authority. God is revealed through the events of salvation history recorded in the Bible.

2. Another view of authority was popular during the Protestant Reformation. Martin Luther, among others, said Jesus Christ was the ultimate standard of authority. This *Christocentric* view said that even the Old Testament had to be read in light of Jesus. Anything that disagreed with the words or spirit of Jesus did not have equal authority with Jesus. The Bible is Scripture because of him.

3. Another position focuses on what happens to the person reading the Bible rather than on the Bible itself. The authority of Scripture here is in what happens to a person today to change his or her life as he or she reads the Bible. What is important is the moment of realizing the point and the claim that God makes as we listen to Scripture. This is a form of *existentialism*.

Word of God

Each of these ways of claiming the authority of the Bible makes some sense. The Bible does have a sense of being inspired. It does assemble around certain pivotal, saving events. It does call readers to hear and make decisions in the present moment. It does center in a decisive way around Jesus Christ. There is something true and valid about each of these approaches. But even taking them all together, does that tell the whole story about what we can believe about the Bible? Or is something still missing?

There is—and we must look back to the Bible itself to find it. We are chasing a slippery eel now, one that the Bible calls the *Word of God.* The Hebrew term for *word (dabar)* means not only word but also deed or thing. It usually refers to some kind of action or event. So, the Word of God is divine action, God busy doing something. And that something is making God known, communicating what God is like and what God's purposes are. This concept is fundamental to the witness of both Old and New Testaments.

By the Word of God, creation appeared, Israel was guided, Jesus was raised. By the Word of God, prophets spoke, Mary trusted, Saul became Paul, and Luther changed the world. By the Word of God, people who have never heard the gospel can read the Bible and be stirred to claim faith.

The Word of God, then, is another helpful way to talk about the Bible's authority as Scripture. The Bible itself is not the Word, but in and through the Bible we hear the Word. Reformers in the sixteenth century also claimed that we hear the Word through preaching, as a sermon reveals the meaning of a biblical passage for the listeners.

The Bible, as the necessary conduit through which the Word of God flows to us, has two aspects: one human and one divine. The Bible is full of the words of real human beings located in particular times and settings. *And* the Bible carries divine freight.

Through it God's Word says something more than what human culture alone can generate.

This approach is another way of reminding ourselves that nothing can contain or limit God. No theory of the Bible's authority can express all that is true about the Word of God. For it is carried into our life by the Holy Spirit, who "blows where it chooses, and you hear the sound of it, but you do not know where it comes from or where it goes" (John 3:8a).

Scripture's Appeal

For more than two thousand years these writings have been at the heart of something almost unexplainable. People all around the world have listened to those words, have said *Yes* to the Spirit's tug, and have become different because of it. Through it all, yesterday and today, those who follow find out in their souls what Scripture declares to all who will listen: that we live by the love, the goodness, the grace of a living, present God.

Adapted from Session 4, "Why Should We Believe the Bible? (continued)," of *Foundations: Basics of the Christian Faith for Youth*, Teacher Book (Copyright © 1988 by Graded Press); Volume 2, pages 20-21.

THE CENTRALITY OF SCRIPTURE

When we try to understand God's message to us and to live life in accordance with the will of God, we turn to the *Scripture* and *tradition* of the church for guidance, to our own *experience* for verification, and to our *reason* for the tools with which to bring Scripture, tradition, and experience together.

Scripture

In many ways the Bible is like a patchwork quilt. It comes to us having been written by many persons in many different times. And yet the multicolored patches form one garment. The experiences that prompted the writing of the Bible were so important to those who lived, told, and wrote about them that it became and remains today a sacred text.

The Bible is sacred because it contains the Word of God. The Bible has stories of history, just as it has poetry and moral and ethical instruction. But the Bible is more than interesting history, beautiful poetry, and important moral lessons. The Bible is sacred because God has chosen to use it as a means of communicating with us.

We might summarize the centrality of the Scripture in these ways:

The Scripture is central because in and through it we meet God. To be sure, the Scripture is the record of how others have met God. We read of Moses meeting God in the burning bush that was not consumed; of Ruth meeting God in a crisis point in her life; of Paul meeting God on the road to Damascus. But as we read, study, and meditate upon the Scripture, God meets us there too and shares the divine nature with us.

The Scripture is central because therein God shares with us the divine plan. The world often seems chaotic to us. Events we experience may make no sense to us. We look for a deeper meaning to life than the simple biological cycle of birth and death. The Scripture teaches us that God has ordered the world for God's own purposes. God has appeared in the world in Jesus of Nazareth "reconciling the world to himself" (1 Corinthians 5:19).

The Scripture is central because through it we understand God's nature. "God so loved the world . . ." is the way John describes God's nature (John 3:16). The God revealed in Jesus Christ is unique among the gods that have been worshiped by humankind throughout its long history. When the volcano erupts on Hawaii, the Christian does not interpret this to mean that the goddess Pele is unhappy with humankind. Terrible things happen in the world, but we know from the Scripture that God's nature is love and that "all things work together for good for those who love God" (Romans 8:28).

The Scripture is central because in it we find all that is necessary for holy living. Holy living is living that is graced by the spiritual gifts of faith, hope, and love. Through the Scripture we gain the spiritual strength required to live in harmony with God's purposes. All persons seek answers to the questions of life: How do I know what is right and wrong? To which goals should I devote my life and energy? How can I fulfill my potential? These are questions the Bible takes seriously and for which it offers answers.

For these reasons the Bible has the central place in our lives and is the basis for all our worship as Christians. If we look closely at the hymns we sing and the prayers we pray, we will find that they all are centered in the biblical message.

The Received Tradition

When Jesus went to the synagogue he read from the Hebrew Scriptures. While these Scriptures were considered sacred texts, they were also part of the tradition into which Jesus was born. So it is with us. Scripture is both sacred text and part of our tradition. The Bible is part of the world into which we are born. It is part of our tradition.

In the church, tradition has enriched the experience of us all. The hymns, prayers, and creeds of the church, while centered in Scripture, have become part of our tradition. When we affirm the creeds, we share across the centuries with those who found in the Scripture the central ideas of the faith now embodied in those timeless statements of faith. We remember the stories of our fathers and mothers in the faith and draw strength from their examples. We sing the hymns of the Wesleys and of countless others both before and after them and rejoice in the traditions of the church that help make us who we are.

Tradition helps us reach beyond the weaknesses of the church in the present and recover the richness of faith expressed in earlier generations. John Wesley believed that the Scripture, especially the idea of scriptural holiness, was not being taught in the church of his time. He offended many churchmen of his day by his method and style of preaching. His conviction about the meaning of Scripture led to the establishment of the Methodist societies in England and, eventually, to the precursor of The United Methodist Church.

Wesley did not reject tradition. Rather he reached beyond his own day to an earlier tradition that for him led to a more fulfilling understanding of the Word of God. The tradition of the church can also enrich our lives and our faith and can help us understand the Scripture for our own time.

Experience

Scripture and tradition present us with an understanding of the world. But surely one of the most important tasks of life, if not *the* most important task, is to develop beliefs that are genuinely our own. Our personal experience is a vital part of that development.

Religious experience seems to be universal, but not all religious experiences are alike. For the Christian, authentic religious experience must be in harmony with the gospel. When we believe God is speaking to us, what we hear must be tested against the basic message of the Scripture. If what we hear is different from the message of Scripture, our experience must be rejected.

When we read about the life of John Wesley, we learn that he was reared in the Christian faith, and knew the Scripture. But it was not until he found what he had learned ringing true in his life that it became a living faith.

One of the great strengths of the Wesleyan movement has been its emphasis on the experience of the Christian in verifying the truth of the Christian faith. Scripture and tradition may teach us that God is love; but if we do not experience God's love as a reality in our lives, those teachings will be difficult to believe.

Human experience varies little from generation to generation. People in every time and place struggle with matters of faith and obedience. In every age there are those for whom life experiences do not strengthen faith in Jesus Christ. Scripture and tradition remind us we are not alone in doubt and

24

uncertainty. Many of the great heroes of the faith had moments of doubt and uncertainty.

Reason

God has given us minds and the power of reason by which we may understand our world and our place in it. Reason is that part of us through which we are able to plan ahead, to learn from mistakes, to understand meanings, and to apply ethical standards to our living. The power of reason has made it possible for persons to walk on the moon, to improve the quality of food products, to discover the basis of disease, and to establish institutions that provide healing and support for persons in special need.

The very fact that we speak of the Scripture as God's Word implies that God chooses to address us as rational beings. Words are uniquely products of rationality. Without reason it would not be possible to hear or to respond to God's Word. Nor would it be possible to examine our lives and our traditions in the light of Scripture.

When we read Scripture, we are enabled by reason to consider the time and place in which the particular passage was written and to reflect on the people and the situation to which it was first addressed. Reason helps us determine the unique relevance of that Scripture for us and for our time. For while God's truth is timeless, every generation must discover how to apply that truth in its time and place. Surely the fundamental truth of the Scripture is that God is love and that we are called to be in loving relationships. It is through reason that we are able to determine just what it means to act lovingly toward the other.

Summary

The life of the Christian is to be lived in response to the gracious love of God. We learn of that love in the Scripture, especially in the Gospel story of the birth, life, ministry, suffering, death, and resurrection of Jesus of Nazareth. We are supported in our faith by the witness of all those who have gone before us and who have shaped the tradition we have received. In our lives, when we know the empowerment of love, we verify in our own experience the truth of the Christian message. In reading the Scripture, in responding to the tradition, and in interpreting our experience we employ the power of reason.

But in all things, reason, experience, and tradition are focused on what God has made known in Scripture.

THE GEOGRAPHY OF PALESTINE

Since the time of the Greek historian Herodotus (fifth century B.C.), the name *Palestine*, among other names, has designated much of the territory along the eastern coast of the Mediterranean Sea.

Under British rule by mandate of the League of Nations (1922–1947), *Palestine* meant roughly the territory south of Mount Hermon as far as the Sinai desert and from the Mediterranean Sea to the Jordan River. The land east of the Jordan to the Syrian and Arabian deserts was called Transjordan or the Hashemite Kingdom of Jordan. Transjordan will be included in this discussion of the geography of Palestine.

The traditional boundaries of Palestine embrace a territory about the size of Vermont, around ten thousand square miles. From Dan to Beersheba is about 145 air miles. In times of expansion, as under King David, when Israelite territory took in southern and central Syria, including Damascus, and reached to the Red Sea on the south, the north-south distance was some 350 air miles. East-west the territory measured about 95 miles.

Palestine lies between the cradles of ancient civilizations: the Tigris-Euphrates river valley (modern Iraq) to the northeast, Egypt to the southwest. Palestine is a land bridge over which the traders and armies of the world have traveled. International commerce gave it prosperity in times of peace, and armies reduced it to ashes in times of war.

The land stretching from the Persian Gulf northwestward up the Tigris-Euphrates valley, through Syria, and down the Phoenician coast to the Sinai desert has been called "the Fertile Crescent." Here there was water enough to sustain settled life and to support international trade, travel, and the movement of armies.

The geography of Palestine is very complex. The mountains, valleys, gorges (rifts), and plateaus run mainly north-south, but also northeast to southwest, northwest to southeast, and in some cases east-west.

With elevations ranging from about 9,200 feet above sea level at the crest of Mount Hermon to about 1,300 feet below sea level at the Dead Sea, climates and flora and fauna vary widely. Houses of mud or even sun-dried brick with straw roofs were adequate in the warm climate of the Jordan Valley. But stone houses roofed with beams of wood overlaid with branches and clay mixed with small stones and furnished with braziers for heating in winter were needed in the hill country. Because of its great diversity of land, climate, peoples, and natural life, Palestine has always been the world in miniature.

1. *The Coastal Plain.* Reaching from Tyre in the north to Gaza in the south, the Coastal Plain is some

130 miles long. It is narrow in the north and broadens out in the south. Some parts of the plain were only lightly settled in biblical times. On the southern end were the five Philistine cities (Gaza, Ashdod, Ashkelon, Gath, Ekron).

South of Tyre the only good natural harbor is at Acco (modern Haifa), just north of Mount Carmel. Herod the Great constructed an artificial harbor at Caesarea (22–10 B.C.) by building a huge breakwater and semicircular seawall into the Mediterranean Sea. Because of the lack of natural harbors, the Hebrews never ventured westward as did the Phoenicians to the north. Commerce by caravans through their territory moved mostly along the Coastal Plain, as did the armies of the ancient world.

2. *The Low Hill Country* (the Shephelah, meaning "lowland") lies between the Coastal Plain and the mountains of Judea. Wide valleys, suited to agriculture, reach among the low limestone hills. The area was a battleground between the Hebrews and the Philistines on the Coastal Plain and offered suitable sites for fortified cities of the contending peoples.

3. *The Central Mountains.* Palestine consists largely of the southern foothills of the Lebanon Mountains. In Lebanon the mountains rise some 6,000 feet above sea level (except for the 9,200 foot Mount Hermon), descend to about 2,000 feet in Samaria (except for the 3,083 and 2,889 foot peaks of Ebal and Gerizim), rise to around 2,600 feet at Jerusalem, and finally fall away to the barren ridges and dunes of the steppe land south of Beersheba (the Negeb). The limestone

mountains, once largely forested, are now mostly barren, with patches of reforestation here and there and pockets of agriculture (olives, figs, wheat, grape vines).

Breaking the north-south mountains and running northwest-southeast are the fertile, near sea-level plains of Megiddo and Jezreel, the latter dropping quickly to the low Jordan Valley. East-west valleys in Samaria (at Dothan and Shechem) and in Judah (at Aijalon, Sorek, and Elah) offer routes from the Coastal Plain into the mountain areas.

4. *The Jordan Valley.* The Jordan Valley is part of the largest geological fault on earth. It begins in Syria and extends into eastern Africa. In the Rift are the Huleh Valley, the Sea of Galilee (Lake Tiberias), the Jordan Valley, the Dead Sea, the Arabah Plain, and the Gulf of Aqabah. The Sea of Galilee is about 695 feet below sea level and the Dead Sea about 1,300 feet below. The average width of the Jordan Valley is about ten miles.

The water of the Sea of Galilee is fresh, but that of the Dead Sea has a high mineral content (sodium chloride, potash, bromine, phosphate, magnesium, calcium, potassium) and is without marine life. Between the Sea of Galilee and the Dead Sea, actually a distance of only about sixty-five miles, the Jordan River's snake-like bed actually meanders for some two hundred miles. In ancient times this area was a jungle and the lair of wild animals. Some tributary rivers flow into the Jordan from the east, and several fords in the Jordan have made east-west travel and commerce possible.

5. *The Transjordan Plateau.* This territory is divided by four main east-west streams (the Yarmuk, the Jabbok, the Arnon, and the Zered) making five definite zones. These are (from north to south) Bashan, Gilead, Ammon, Moab, and Edom.

Bashan is good pasture land, with abundant black basalt for house building.

Gilead, heavily forested in ancient times, also offers good pasture land. Its trees apparently produced a sort of medicinal "balm" valued in antiquity (Jeremiah 8:22).

Ammon forms the center of the eastern highlands, with its capital city at the headwater of the Jabbok River (Rabbah, now Amman). The Ammonites and the Hebrews were often locked in bitter warfare.

Moab, on whose plains Israel camped before entering the Promised Land (Numbers 35:1; Deuteronomy 1:5), is somewhat high (at points over 3,000 feet) and comparatively well-watered. Moab has produced wheat and barley, sheep and goats, and was sometimes prosperous when there was a famine in Judah (Ruth 1:1). Hostility broke out frequently through the centuries between the Hebrews and the Moabites.

Edom, meaning "red" because of the reddish sandstone of the area, was a source of copper in antiquity. Its wise men were noted for their wisdom (Jeremiah 49:7; Obadiah 1:8). The inhabitants depended largely for their sustenance on the caravans that passed through their borders.

The "King's Highway," a major public road and international caravan route, ran the full length of the Transjordan Plateau from Damascus in the north to the Gulf of Aqabah in the south and brought wealth to the towns and areas through which it passed.

In latitude, Palestine falls in a line with Georgia (United States). In general its climate has two seasons: a rainy winter, with snow in the Lebanon mountains and occasionally in Jerusalem, and a long, dry summer. The early (or "former") rains, which soften the ground for plowing, fall in October and November. The heavy rains come in December—February. And the late (or "latter") rains, which ripen the crops, descend in March and April.

The rain clouds come from the West. Annual rainfall often reaches sixty inches in parts of Lebanon, forty inches in upper Galilee, twenty-six inches at Jerusalem, ten to fifteen inches in the region between Hebron and Beersheba, eight inches in the Negeb to the south, and five inches in southern Transjordan.

If rains do not come at the right time in the right amounts, crops fail and famine may result (1 Kings 17:1; 18:1-2). Prayers for rain and rain-inducing ceremonies (Zechariah 10:1; Joel 2:23) were an important part of Israel's religious and economic life. The prophets of Israel strongly contended that the Lord Yahweh, not the Canaanite Baal, controlled the rains and the crops the rains nourished (Amos 4:7-8; Hosea 2:5,8; Jeremiah 5:23-24).

By our standards Palestine is a land poorly endowed, on the whole. The central portion of the country consists of limestone hills and mountains without much depth of soil. Harbors along its coast are few and inadequate. The cut-up, rocky, and generally arid ground doomed its inhabitants to hard labor for a minimal level of existence.

But more devastating than lack of water and good soil for the life of Palestine's people has been the almost incessant warfare and destruction the country's location and physical character have brought. Since Palestine forms a land bridge between the great civilizations of the Middle East, it was inevitable that it should be at the mercy of their peoples in times of international expansion and conflict. Alliance with one or another of the dominant powers, in order to gain security, often ended in Palestine's destruction along with that of its defeated ally. In addition, in times of famine marauding peoples from the desert to the east and south of Transjordan pressed with devastating results into the more fertile corridor to the west.

The great diversity in the surface of Palestine has always made political, economic, religious, and social unification difficult. Thus a common front against external enemies was often hindered by local squabbles and indifference.

To summarize, security, water, bread, and cultural,

political, and religious unity have been dominant problems of this little land.

The ancient Hebrews looked on their land as "a good land" (Deuteronomy 8:7-8). Compared to the desert areas in which Israel wandered for a generation in the time of Moses, the characterization is justified. But life on this international bridge has always been difficult and insecure. The Promised Land was no Garden of Eden; hence, seers and prophets looked forward to the coming of that Garden in the latter days.

MAJOR THEMES IN SCRIPTURE

Where do we look for major themes in *Scripture*? How will we know what is major when we find it?

Our first guide is *tradition*, which simply means what the church has taught with some consistency throughout its history.

We also use *reason* as we examine Scripture and tradition. We ask questions, challenge conventional answers, and balance rival conclusions.

Finally, we find that our beliefs interact with our *experience*. How does a belief influence our experience? How do our experiences reflect on a belief?

The scriptural themes outlined here have stood the test of hundreds of years of experience in the tradition of the church. They have been tested by reason and lived out in experience.

God: Creator and Redeemer

This Good World. A foundation for everything else we believe is our faith in God as Creator. We and our world owe our existence to the constant flow of the creative and sustaining energy of God. Indeed, now that we are learning more about the mysteries of space, we may say that whatever other worlds may exist out there, whatever extraterrestrial creatures may live in whatever strange worlds, they, too, owe their existence to the same God we acknowledge as "maker of heaven and earth, and of all things, visible and invisible" (The Nicene Creed).

The Bible begins with two stories of Creation: Genesis 1:1–2:4a and 2:4b-25. Over and over in Genesis 1 we find the words: "And God saw that it was good." We are impressed that, no matter how bad things may look, the world we live in is fundamentally good. The profound importance and value of the relationship between male and female and the integrity of human sexuality are stressed (Genesis 1:27-31; 2:21-25).

Psalm 8 is a moving affirmation of the wonder of creation and our place in it, acknowledging our dependence upon our Creator.

In a poem of haunting beauty the prophet Isaiah sings of the wonder of God's being and the intimacy of God's presence with us (Isaiah 40).

The Human Creature: Special and Spoiled. We humans are a part of creation. Contemporary concern with ecology reminds us of this fact. True, we are given "dominion" over the rest of creation (Genesis 1:26, 28), which surely means that we are to respect and use our world for our common good.

But we are also different from the rest of creation. We are made "in the image of God" (Genesis 1:27). Tradition has identified this image in many ways.

One basic understanding is that we are created with a special relationship to God, a relationship of responsibility and response-ability, as one scholar put it. Rooted in this relationship are the creative gifts that make human life beautiful, gifts that we all share in some measure.

We are special—and always will be. But we have spoiled it. The story of Creation continues into the story of the Fall (Genesis 3). Adam and Eve, endowed with the freedom to respond to God's will, choose to go their own way. That's precisely our story.

What was their sin? Basically, pride, self-will. And note: we all exercise the same proud self-will (Romans 3:23).

The consequence is alienation. First, from God against whom we have rebelled; then from nature: we are driven out of the Garden. And tragically, from each other: man from woman, later brother from brother (as Cain from Abel, Genesis 4:1-8).

God's Concern for Humanity: Covenant. The bad news is our rebellion. The good news is God's response. God is troubled by our misbehavior and must deal with it. But God never gives up on us (Genesis 6:1-8). Our Creator is also our Redeemer.

One of the most beautiful insights of the Old Testament is that God takes the initiative to form a covenant, a special kind of contract, with humanity. Essentially what God says is this: I really do love you and do not want to let you go on the way you are. If you will just listen to me and obey me, I will see that you receive the blessings I really intend for you.

So God made a covenant with Abraham (Genesis 12:1-3; 22:15-18); and renewed it with Moses (Exodus 2:24; 3). We note that this covenant, made with Israel, is also for the good of "all the families of the earth."

Jeremiah dreamed of a "new covenant," a spiritual deepening of God's redeeming relationship with humanity (Jeremiah 31:31-34).

The new covenant is given a still deeper meaning by Jesus. On the eve of his death, he established a new form of this covenant with his disciples and through them with us (Matthew 26:26-29; Mark 14:22-25; Luke 22:17-19; also 1 Corinthians 11:23-26).

The term *new covenant* is familiar to us as "New Testament."

God of Goodness and Mercy. The God who is revealed to us in the Old Testament is marked by a very special character. The God of Israel is different from the gods of Israel's neighbors and the gods worshiped in other civilizations. Yahweh, as Israel's God is named, is a holy God and demands holiness of the chosen people. Moreover, God demands exclusive loyalty and worship. That is what is meant when it is said that God is "jealous."

But—and the wonder of the divine character deepens—this holy God is also a God of mercy. God loves the human creatures; that is why God enters into a covenant to redeem them. And this quality of mercy, translated also as "steadfast love," is the deepest mark of the divine character.

The joining of goodness and mercy is affirmed consistently. When God demands obedience, the promise of mercy is offered as well (see Exodus 20:4-6; Deuteronomy 7:6-11).

The psalmist sings of God's mercy, "steadfast love," and invites us to rejoice in this faith (Psalm 100).

One of the loveliest expressions of God's love is found in the writings of Hosea. His wife had cheated on him, as we have been unfaithful to God. But Hosea could not stop loving his wife and realized that, in much the same way, God cannot give us up.

God Is Love.   It is in Jesus Christ that the love of God is most fully revealed and expressed. This is our distinctive Christian belief.

Jesus, of course, was brought up with the Hebrew faith in the mercy of God. In his own teaching Jesus reaffirmed this faith and added a new dimension to it. Not only does God love us disobedient humans, but God actively seeks us in our erring ways.

So Jesus told the story of the shepherd who "goes after" his lost sheep, the woman sweeping her house to "search carefully" for her lost savings. And the story that everyone loves: the prodigal son whose return is celebrated by the father who "was filled with compassion; he ran and put his arms around him and kissed him" (Luke 15).

These stories were told in response to the frequent

criticism aimed at Jesus. He deliberately sought out the social outcast, the disinherited. His response on another such occasion is direct and powerful: "The Son of Man came to seek out and to save the lost" (Luke 19:10).

The followers of Jesus deepened this striking statement by saying, not only did Jesus teach the seeking love of God, Jesus is the expression of God's outgoing, saving love. John 3:16, perhaps the most loved verse in the New Testament, affirms such faith very clearly. Verse 17 states the purpose of God's radical action.

The Triune God. We have spoken of God as Father and God as Son. The writers of the Old Testament could not have said this. Only in the New Testament is such a faith affirmed.

The Hebrew faith is strictly monotheistic. There is only one God, the God of Israel. Jesus and his disciples, of course, believed this.

The Christian church clings to the belief in one God. But the church also recognizes that God is experienced in more than one way. The early Christians sensed that, in Jesus, God was approaching them in a special way. And after Jesus died and rose again, they began to say, "God sent His Son." The God whom they knew as Father had come to them as Son.

Already they were stretching their faith about the one God. But more was to follow. Soon they would experience God as Holy Spirit; and they would have to find new language to use about God.

The writers of the New Testament did not develop a full doctrine about the Trinity. But they used language that suggested the creeds that would follow: Matthew 28:19; 2 Corinthians 13:14. They gave us the raw material out of which later generations of Christians formed the doctrine of the Trinity: One God in Three Persons.

The Person and Work of Christ

Incarnation. The startling statement of John 3:16-17 raises two questions about Jesus. Who was he? And what did he do? The answers given in the New Testament grew into two of the great doctrines of the church: Incarnation and Atonement.

Incarnation means that in Jesus of Nazareth God entered human history in a unique way. God became a human being. God was incarnate—enfleshed—in Jesus.

Every writer of the New Testament affirmed this statement about Incarnation. They did so in different ways and with different images: in the Gospel stories about what Jesus said and did, in sermons recorded in Acts, in reflection on who Jesus was in the Epistles, and in the great vision of a new world found in Revelation. Each document, in its own way, affirms Jesus as Lord (the word used for God in the Old Testament) and Christ (Messiah).

41

Perhaps the most eloquent statement of this faith is in what is known as the Prologue to John's Gospel (John 1:1-18). The central affirmation is in verse 14: The Word (which in verse 1 is identified with God) became flesh (an authentic human being).

And if we ask—as we must—what God intends by this mysterious venture, the answer is in verses 17 and 18. Jesus Christ opens up a new way to relate to God (not law but grace). Jesus Christ has made God fully known.

Atonement. The second question is: What did Jesus do? The answer to that question is expressed in the doctrine of the Atonement.

Atonement means the restoration of our relationship with God. We have been at odds; now we may be at one. And the radical assertion of our faith is that this restoration is not our doing; it is God's act on our behalf.

The suffering and death of Jesus is the central deed of Atonement. All through the New Testament is the recognition of Jesus' death on the cross as the saving act of God. In this death God does what is necessary to restore our relationship with God and to heal our relationship with other people.

Several images of Atonement are used by the writers of the New Testament. One is *expiation* (Romans 3:25; 1 John 2:2; 4:9-10). This difficult term means something like cleansing from evil so a person will be able to approach God.

Another image is the legal term, *justification.* We

are guilty. We know it, but cannot do anything about our guilt. God takes on our guilt and freely forgives us (John 3:16-17; Romans 5:8. Ephesians 1:7 adds *redemption*, as in the freeing of slaves).

Perhaps the most beautiful image is *reconciliation*. We are alienated from God and defensive about it. God, whom we have offended, makes the advances to us, to break down our defensiveness and to heal the relationship. Second Corinthians 5:19 is the direct statement of this remarkable affirmation.

Resurrection. The work of Jesus does not end with his death. Crucifixion issues in Resurrection. Here again is a central unanimous witness of the writers of the New Testament.

The Gospels tell the story. Each writer tells it in his own way and recounts events as he recalls them. But the witness is clear: God raised Jesus from the dead.

The sermons recorded in Acts—the earliest Christian witness to the alien world—reaffirm this faith (Acts 2:24, 32; 17:31). The emphasis is always that "God raised him up." Resurrection is not the bubbling up of human potential. It is God's redeeming act: the winning of life over death.

The same refrain runs through the Epistles. In 1 Corinthians 15:3-8, Paul gives the earliest written account of the event on which our faith is based. And he reasons decisively from this event. The argument is complicated but the conclusion is clear: our hope is solidly based on God's victory over death in the resurrection of Jesus.

Paul draws a helpful inference from this faith. The same energy by which God raised Jesus from the dead is available to us to enable us to defeat the deadly influences that would ruin our lives and to achieve a new quality of life. (Romans 8:11 is one statement of this.)

The Healing of Humanity: Amazing Grace. Reflection on what we have said about the person and work of Jesus Christ will make it clear that all this is God's redeeming action on our behalf. It is the expression of divine grace: the outgoing, sacrificial love of God.

The Creator and Redeemer moves continually toward humanity at ever deeper levels. What was first glimpsed in the covenant (God's concern for humanity), what was sung about by poets and prophets (the divine mercy), is now fully expressed in the self-giving, suffering love of God, given in Jesus Christ.

This amazing grace is the sole basis of our hope for healing. Acceptance of this grace-full gift is the key to release from our guilt and its frustrations, release into free and glad living. A careful reading of Romans 3:23-25 will yield a strong statement of this faith. (See also Ephesians 2:8-9.)

John Wesley recovered a beautiful term to express the mystery of God's free gift of love. He spoke of "prevenient grace." That means the love that seeks us out when we are lost (as the shepherd searching for the sheep). It means that, even when we are angry and alienated, God tries to win us back

44

(reconciliation). Even when we are unaware of it, God is trying to get through to us. And when we finally do accept the gift, we sense that it is because God has consistently been trying to persuade us to do so.

Justification by Faith. We admit, however reluctantly, that we are sinners. We not only do wrong things, we are the kind of persons who are capable of stupid and destructive thoughts and actions. How can we be forgiven, not just for our mistakes but for our stance?

The Christian reply is the radical doctrine known as *justification by faith*: we are forgiven by accepting God's freely offered gift of grace. Unfortunately, we tend to hide this unexpected, maybe even uncomfortable, answer in a list of duties and obligations. So our practice becomes an attempt to earn forgiveness by obeying the supposed requirements.

Periodically, then, the startling affirmation of free grace has to be recovered. That was a prime aspect of the Protestant Reformation. Martin Luther rediscovered Paul's amazing statement in Romans 3:28. That verse became the watchword of the Reformation and of every Protestant church that emerged from the Reformation.

John Wesley was another who recovered in his day the doctrine of justification by faith. His preaching had the same igniting, renewing effect. To put it in Wesley's own terms: when we accept "prevenient grace," it becomes "justifying grace." We are assured of our forgiveness and are led into new dimensions of life.

Faith, then, is the acceptance of God's gift. Trying to earn God's favor is frustrating; we are tied up in knots. Rather, we open ourselves to God, who has already been trying to reach us; and we trust the steadfast love that we know as grace.

Faith and Works. Paul was quite specific: we are justified by faith "apart from works prescribed by the law" (Romans 3:28). Luther underscored it, saying, "by faith alone." This statement of belief raises an interesting question. Does that mean that, once we are saved, we may behave as we please?

This question seems to have arisen right at the beginning of Paul's ministry. So in one of his earliest letters, to the Galatians, he had to write quite firmly. We are free from the harsh dominance of the law; but we are not freed in order to do as we please. We are released into the deeper law of love (Galatians 5:13-15).

James stressed the importance of living out our faith in works. James put it bluntly: "Show me your faith apart from your works, and I by my works will show you my faith" (2:18).

Surely it is not either/or. Faith draws us into faithfulness. But we must be clear that obedience is not a grim effort to earn forgiveness. Our works of love are a glad response to God's freely given love.

46

The Holy Spirit and The Church

The Spirit of Power, Truth, Love. Our Christian life begins with forgiveness. Where do we go from here? We feel the imperative to love. But how do we go about that? At this point the New Testament offers us a gracious new resource: the presence and power of the Holy Spirit.

Pentecost was the occasion of a definitive experience in the lives of the disciples (Acts 2:1-4). Jesus had promised them that, after he left, the Holy Spirit would come to them (Acts 1:4-5; John 16:7). And, he added, they would "receive power" (Acts 1:8). We believe we share the same promise: God can be present to us, at the deepest level of our being, to heal, motivate, and stimulate our growth.

John records Jesus as speaking of the Spirit in an impressive series of images (John 14:15-17, 25-26; 15:26-27; 16:7-15). The Holy Spirit is the Spirit of Truth who will lead us into further truth, the Counselor who will stimulate and sustain our growth.

Paul writes extensively of the "gifts of the Spirit" (1 Corinthians 12) and more intimately of the "fruit of the Spirit" (Galatians 5:22). The principal gift or fruit of the Spirit is the capacity to love (1 Corinthians 13).

John Wesley put great emphasis on our experience of the Holy Spirit as the means to achieve excellence and fulfilment in our Christian living. He spoke of "Christian perfection," the fullness of spiritual maturity. He spoke of "sanctification" as the process of growing toward that maturity. All of this is the fruit of our openness to the deep presence of the Holy Spirit. Christian perfection is also a gift, the working out of God's grace in our lives. Just as God calls us through prevenient grace and redeems us through justifying grace, so also God leads us to grow in our faith (to "go on to perfection") through "sanctifying grace."

The Community of the Spirit. This account of Christian experience is still incomplete. It is personal, but it cannot be solitary. We individuals do not live alone; we need community. And the New Testament offers a special fulfillment of that need: the church.

Where Paul writes most extensively of the Spirit, he writes also of the Church (1 Corinthians 11–14). We tend to think of "joining" the church. Paul speaks as if we are "called into" the church to form a community of the Spirit.

The phrase *the body of Christ* is perhaps the best-known image for the church (1 Corinthians 12). As individuals we are bound together in an organic union. We have many different gifts of the Spirit, all of which are essential to the total life of the community. We live and work together "for the common good" (verse 7). So "there is one body and one Spirit" (Ephesians 4:4; read also 4:1-16).

The earliest forms of congregational organization and practice were simple; but as the church grew, they became more complex. Always, however, the function of the church was clear, and still is: first, to nurture our Christian experience ("building up the body of Christ"); and at the same time to equip us "for the work of ministry" (Ephesians 4:12).

The Sacraments. From the beginning of their new life in Christ, Christians met together for fellowship and worship (Acts 2:42, 46; Hebrews 10:23-25). They began with practices already familiar to them, in the life of the synagogues, and gradually gave them new meaning.

Some forms of worship quickly gained special importance, and came to be known as sacraments. There are differences about just what should be called a sacrament, but most Protestants recognize two, perhaps because they are definitely rooted in the New Testament itself.

Baptism was a Jewish practice, as we see in the ministry of John the Baptizer and Jesus' acceptance of the rite (Matthew 3; Mark 1:4-11; Luke 3:2-22; John 1:6-8, 19-34). However, baptism in the name of Jesus (Acts 2:38) and in the name of the Trinity (Matthew 28:19) gave the rite an entirely new meaning. Fundamentally, baptism is the sign of the saving grace of God at work in our lives, and of our entry into the community of the Spirit.

Holy Communion is the second sacrament of the church, instituted by Jesus himself at the Last Supper. The story is told in the Gospels and in Paul's even earlier record (1 Corinthians 11:23-25). This Lord's Supper, or Eucharist as it is also known, has become the central act of Christian worship. The whole Christian gospel is affirmed in this sacrament: all that we mean by Incarnation, Atonement, justification, sanctification, and the hope of eternal life.

The People of God. Another image of the church is *the people of God* (1 Peter 2:9-10). This image, of course, reflects back on the understanding of Israel as God's chosen people; and affirms that as Christians we are called to be the newly constituted people of God.

The Greek word for people is *laos*. From this comes our word *laity*, and this word indicates exactly what is meant by the church. The church is not the clergy, or the conference, or the synod, not the institutional forms. The church is the people of God. Two phrases help us understand what that means.

The priesthood of believers is a great phrase from the Protestant Reformation. It affirms that every person can come directly to God in faith. Every believer is a priest.

The ministry of the laity means that the laity are the ministers of Christ in secular society. The work of the body of Christ in the world is done by the "members" of the body. The ministry of Christ to society is carried out by the people, the laity, "ordained" to this ministry by their baptism.

What is our responsibility in society? In a word—a demanding word—to love our neighbors. So Jesus tells the searching story of the good Samaritan (Luke

10:25-37). Paul also endorses the central importance of love (Galatians 5:13-15; Romans 13:8-10). We are called to the continuing task of finding ways to implement this "royal law."

Dimensions of Hope

The Kingdom of God. One of the impressive marks of the teaching of Jesus is his extensive use of the term "the kingdom of God." However, its meaning turns out to be quite complicated. Some persons have tried to identify the church and the kingdom. Others have thought of the kingdom as a just social order. Neither interpretation seems to fit the evidence.

The word *kingdom* means rule or reign. Two consistent aspects of God's sovereignty are that God does rule over the universe and over history, whether we admit it or not; but the full effect of God's rule depends on our accepting and obeying it.

So the burden of the prophets' message was that, though Israel theoretically acknowledged God as their King, their habitual disobedience could only end in disaster (Amos 7:7-9).

Jesus adds a new note; he affirms that in his own presence and ministry, the rule of God is present in a new way (dramatically stated in Luke 17:20-21). Jesus asserts this in a series of sayings about the end and outcome of history that are quite troubling (see Mark 13).

In the meantime, we have to come to terms with the sovereignty of God. Perhaps the best simple word is Jesus' exhortation: Let it be the top priority of your life to be ruled by God (see Matthew 6:33).

The Coming Kingdom. The writers of Scripture (Old and New Testaments) are remarkably confident that, no matter how we humans behave, God will ultimately assert the divine rule. The God who established the covenant will be faithful to that commitment. And ultimately, not only Israel but "all the families of the earth" will be blessed (Genesis 12:1-3).

This belief issued at last in the prophet Isaiah's beautiful vision of the messianic kingdom. No matter how disobedient we humans may be, God is faithful and will establish a rule of goodness and mercy (Isaiah 2:1-4; 9:2-7; 11:1-9). This vision has fascinated us ever since it was first promised. Will it happen by historical progress? Or is it to be realized only "beyond history"? The ultimate answer is in the hands of God, and we therefore can be confident of the answer.

The Revelation to John is another beautiful, though often puzzling, statement of God's ultimate rule. We must be careful not to use it as a basis for predicting history, as we use charts and graphs to predict the weather. The heart of John's vision is the assurance that no matter what happens in history, God will ultimately affirm the divine sovereignty.

Handel makes us sing it: "He shall reign for ever and ever" (see Revelation 11:15). John assures us that we dare hope to be part of that kingdom: "They

[God's people] shall reign forever and ever" (Revelation 22:5).

Our Father's House. The question of our personal destiny is basic to our human experience. What happens to us when we die?

In the New Testament our faith is personalized. Jesus joined the Pharisees in affirming the resurrection (Mark 12:18-27). His further personal reflections have become a treasured part of our belief: "In my Father's house there are many dwelling places. . . . I go to prepare a place for you. . . . I will come again and will take you to myself" (John 14:2-3; see also verse 27).

Paul, trained as a Pharisee, also believed in the resurrection of the dead (Acts 23:6; 26:8). Then he added a Christian dimension by affirming that the resurrection of Jesus is the decisive evidence for the validity of such faith (1 Corinthians 15:12-20).

Paul personalized our hope in his thoughtful insight that we will be endowed with a "spiritual body" for the transcendent life in our Father's house (1 Corinthians 15:35-38, 42-44). But our hope is not simply personal; the house itself will be transformed. So John envisioned "a new heaven and a new earth" (Revelation 21:1). Paul put it more daringly: the entire cosmos will be released into the fulfillment of God's eternal purpose (Romans 8:18-25).

CANONIZATION AND TRANSLATION

What is a canon of Scripture? Why is it important? How did we get it?

The word *canon* comes from a Greek word that means "measuring reed." When we use the word in connection with Scripture, we mean that these books are a measure, or standard, for faith and life. Canonization is the process by which these particular books came to be regarded as a standard. The canon of Scripture, our Bible, was developed by the people of God in response to the need of the church.

The Scripture of Jesus and the first-century church was the Hebrew Scripture, what we call the Old Testament. For nearly one hundred years, the Hebrew Scripture was the sufficient canon for the church. Then people began to ask questions: Is this enough? What about Jesus? How do we live out our new faith in a world that tempts us to be unfaithful?

Paul's letters were the first part of our New Testament to be written. Because the letters helped answer questions about faith and life, they were saved, copied, collected. By A.D. 95, some Christians were using Paul's letters as Scripture.

Many accounts were written to record what Jesus said and did, and what Jesus' life, death, and resurrection mean for Christians. We know of about a dozen gospels that were written in these early years, but only Matthew, Mark, Luke, and John ever had any real status as gospels in the church. Other Christian writings also appeared—letters, sermons, apocalypses, teachings.

So why did the church decide to develop a New Testament? No one woke up one morning and decided the church needed a canon. Rather, the canon developed in response to pressures from outside the church and from felt needs from the inside.

The canon developed in part because of needs and pressures inside the church. What was right belief? The church defined right belief in "The Rule of Faith"—what we would call creeds. Writings that helped define and support the Rule of Faith became standards, or canons. They were known as apostolic because they preserved the teaching and the tradition of the apostles. This process was the positive side of canonization.

The canon developed in part because of pressures from outside. Many books were written that claimed to be Christian teaching. Someone, somehow, had to decide if these books contained the apostolic teaching. This process was the negative side of canonization. Sometime around A.D. 150, a man named Marcion drew up a list of books that he defined as a canon. His list included ten letters of

Paul and the Gospel of Luke. He rejected the Old Testament because he thought the Creator was not the God of Jesus Christ. When Marcion's list appeared, the church had to think seriously about which books were authoritative.

The church did not respond by calling together a committee to decide. No one had the power to do that. But there was universal agreement on several points in response to Marcion. First, the church believed that the God of the Old Testament was also the God of Jesus Christ. Therefore, the Old Testament was authoritative for faith and life in the church. Second, there was a move toward four Gospels as a standard for faith. Third, other letters were held to be as authoritative as those of Paul. These included what we call First Peter and First John—and for some churches books such as Barnabas, First Clement, and Hermas.

Irenaeus, a bishop in southern France (about A.D. 185) was the first writer to indicate there was a "New Testament," that is, a recognized collection of writings equal in authority and value to the Old Testament. But Irenaeus's collection still did not include all the books we list in our New Testament. Books such as Hebrews, James, Second Peter, Jude, and Revelation were found on some lists of the canon and not on others.

Then came an event that may have been decisive for the process of canonization. In A.D. 303, during the last great persecution, the emperor Diocletian ordered that all the Scriptures be destroyed and anyone who did not surrender the Scriptures was to be killed. Now the question of the canon became personal. Which books were sacred enough to die for?

After Diocletian's persecution, church councils began to define the canon. The oldest known list of New Testament books exactly like ours today was included in a letter Bishop Athanasius of Alexandria sent to his churches in 367. A council held in Rome in 382 gave a complete list of the canonical books of both the Old Testament and the New Testament.

The books we call the Apocrypha were included as a part of the canon for most of the church's history. At the time of the Protestant Reformation, Luther declared the books of the Apocrypha as secondary and not to be counted equal with the authoritative ones. The Roman Catholic Council of Trent in 1546 declared the Apocrypha to be an authoritative part of the canon. Protestants in general have looked on the Apocrypha as secondary and, until recently, did not include it in printed Bibles. In the last thirty years, Protestants have shown more interest in the books of the Apocrypha, without considering them authoritative.

English Versions of the Bible

Translations of parts of the Bible into the Anglo-Saxon language appeared as early as A.D. 700, but the first complete Bible in English did not appear until 1382. John Wycliffe translated the Bible to put it into the hands of the laity. His was the only English Bible in use for over 150 years. Wycliffe's Bible was based on the Latin and did not use any older texts.

Between 1525 and 1535, William Tyndale's translation appeared. Tyndale had the advantage of access to Greek and Hebrew manuscripts, including Erasmus' Greek New Testament of 1514. Tyndale also had the advantage of the printing press, which made it possible to spread copies of the Bible far and wide at a relatively cheap price. Tyndale's Bible had a great influence on the King James Bible and on the development of English as a literary language. Tyndale was killed before he finished translating the entire Bible.

The first complete printed English Bible was that of Miles Coverdale (1535) who used Tyndale's translation as the foundation of his own. Other early English Bibles based on Tyndale's work were the Matthew Bible (1537), the Great Bible, so called because of its size (1539), the Geneva Bible (1560), and the Bishop's Bible (1568). The Geneva Bible was widely read among the people, while the Great Bible was usually read in church. The Douai version of 1610-11 was a Roman Catholic translation from Latin into English.

The King James Bible of 1611 is one of the masterpieces of English literature. It was translated from Greek and Hebrew, with the Bishop's Bible as the standard of translation. In spite of its rank as a treasure of the English language and the love it has stirred for over 350 years, the King James Version also has its weaknesses. One Greek or Hebrew word was translated several different ways. Parallel passages in the Gospels were translated differently, so it was hard to see relationships. Sometimes a translation obscured the meaning of a verse. The Greek and Hebrew texts used by the translators were not as good as texts we know today.

The English Revised Version (1881-85) and the American Standard Version (1901) were revisions aimed at correcting the more obvious mistakes of the King James. These versions used better Greek texts than the King James Version. In spite of having a more accurate text, these versions were widely criticized for daring to revise the Authorized (King James) Version.

The Revised Standard Version (1946, 1952) was a revision based on superior Greek texts, new knowledge of the Greek vocabulary and grammar of the New Testament, and the changes in the English language between 1611 and 1946. It soon became the authorized Bible of much of American Christianity.

The New Revised Standard Version recognizes changes in biblical scholarship and in the English language since 1952. Scholars know more about ancient languages. There are more—and older— manuscripts from which to work. The discovery of the Dead Sea Scrolls, for example, meant that for some books of the Old Testament, we now have manuscripts one thousand years older than any previously used. It is important that the Bible be translated accurately from the best ancient texts. In addition, the English language has changed rapidly in the last fifty years. Words have changed in meaning; new words have appeared. So a standard translation needs to keep up with modern as well as with ancient languages. The New Revised Standard Version is, as nearly as possible, a literal translation of early manuscripts. It is also a free translation wherever necessary to be sure the meaning in English is the same as in Greek or Hebrew.

Other translations and paraphrased editions abound. Two of the most popular translations are *Today's English Version* or the *Good News Bible* as it is commonly called, and the *New International Version*. The TEV was originally developed in 1966 for people for whom English was a second language. It has a limited vocabulary, avoids ecclesiastical terms and is illustrated by line drawings.

The *New International Version*, published in 1978 was prepared by an international group of scholars. It is a very popular edition of the Bible and is less free in its translation than the *Good News Bible*.

Unquestionably, the most popular paraphrased edition today is Kenneth Taylor's *Living Bible, Paraphrased* (1971). It is a mixture of commentary and translation. Dr. Bruce Metzger, noted New Testament scholar says, "a paraphrase tells the reader what the Bible *means*, whereas a literal translation tells what the Bible *says*.

The Holy Spirit

The story of canonization and translation of the Bible may appear to be only a record of reaction to outside events, taking votes, deciding what is authoritatively God's Word, and what is not. The story is all of that, of course. It is also a story of careful scholarship, of treasure hunts for ancient manuscripts and of much time spent in dictionaries.

But the story of canonization and translation also has another layer of meaning, one that is far more profound than the public story. The church has always believed it embarked on the process of canonization and translation under the guidance of the Holy Spirit. We believe God inspired the writing of the Scriptures. We believe God inspired the process of selection of the books that would become Scripture. We believe God was at work in the studies of grammar, vocabulary, and ancient manuscripts that led to the translation of Scripture into the language of the people.

How God worked in those arenas we do not understand. When we try to describe God's actions, words fall short. We disagree with one another over what inspiration means. But we believe, with all our differences, that God was active in the process.

HOW TO STUDY A BIBLE PASSAGE

The Bible is the church's book. Therefore we call the Bible *Scripture*. The Bible is the authoritative guidebook for the church. But many people in the church have trouble claiming the Bible as their own. "It's hard to understand." "It's so complex that we're intimidated."

How can you get past those roadblocks? How can you recover your own foundational book? Part of the answer is to learn how to study Bible passages in some depth. It is not a simple matter. But almost anyone can improve their skill, if they work at it. Once you learn questions to ask about a Bible passage and where to look for help in answering those questions, you are off and running. The more passages you examine and the more you become familiar with tools of Bible study, the more skillful you become in unlocking the message of the Bible.

What Is the Bible Passage You Are Studying?

You may have selected a passage for any one of a hundred reasons. Maybe you saw a biblical quotation on a billboard or in a book. Maybe a passage you heard in church has stuck in your mind. Maybe somebody in the neighborhood or at school or at work asked you (or told you) something about a passage. Maybe you have been searching the Bible for a particular topic and a concordance has directed you to the passage at hand. Or maybe you are trying to read through a book of the Bible and you've found you need to break up the reading into smaller blocks.

Is it a very short passage, say, a few verses? Is it a longer passage, say an entire chapter, or a portion of a chapter? There are no hard and fast rules about the proper length of passage to study. But as a rule of thumb, you might ask: "Do I have a complete thought here?" Sometimes a complete thought is encapsulated in a single verse; seldom in less than a verse; often in more than a verse. Sometimes the paragraph or stanza breaks will give you clues. Sometimes the flow of a story will dictate the right focus. (It wouldn't make sense, for instance, to study only half a parable of Jesus.) Sometimes you need a whole chapter to have a complete thought. Make the best judgment you can and then press on. Later steps will help you know whether you have set the boundaries of a passage fairly.

Read the Passage Carefully, Word-for-Word

The most important step in any type of Bible study is to read the biblical text itself as if you were seeing it for the first time. As Robin Maas, founder of the Lay

Resource Center at Wesley Theological Seminary, points out: "the single greatest obstacle to understanding scripture is the sincere conviction on the part of the reader that he or she already knows what the text means simply because it sounds so familiar." That presumption short-circuits the power of the Bible to challenge and to provoke us.

Take as an example Jesus' parable of the good Samaritan (Luke 10:29-37). Who is the neighbor in this story? Most people would answer, "the man who was beaten and left half-dead." From that answer to the generalization that our neighbor is anyone in need is an easy step. That principle may be sound, but it misses some of the punch in this parable. Look at the text again. The neighbor is actually the Samaritan who rescued the beaten man. Think how that idea, a Jew accepting aid from a despised Samaritan, must have shocked Jewish ears. It would be bad enough to be left helpless but even worse to be utterly dependent on the compassion of one's enemy, or so the situation must have seemed to Jesus' listeners. The message about neighbor-love is richer than most of us suppose. And we miss that deeper meaning unless we carefully discover what the biblical text really says.

So as you read the passage, jot down any words or phrases that catch your eye as potential keys to what the passage is saying. Include any terms that you are not familiar with.

Investigate the Key Terms

Many of the terms used in the Bible are deceptive. You think you know what they mean, but you may miss the richer connotations of the original Hebrew or Greek. So a theological wordbook is an essential Bible study tool. One of the best is *A Theological Word Book of the Bible*, edited by Alan Richardson (Macmillan, 1962).

Take an example. Under the entry for "know, knowledge" you find that the Hebrew term translated as *know* means much more than intellectual knowledge. It means to *have experience* of something or someone. To know God, then means much more than to know information or theories about God; it means that you intimately experience God in your life.

The world the Bible describes is in many respects an unfamiliar world. It is strange because it is unknown. As a careful reader you will not want to gloss over that unfamiliar character, to assume too quickly that you know what was going on in those ancient days. Bible dictionaries can help. More like small-scale encyclopedias than traditional dictionaries, Bible dictionaries have a wealth of information about the people, events, ideas, and books of the Bible.

Examine the Pharisees as one example. Many people have an image of the Pharisees as the bad guys. But a quick look in a Bible dictionary reveals that the Pharisees were in many respects the moral and religious exemplars of their society. Many among them were much like the Christian pillars of our churches today—thoroughly respectable, good, decent, and God-fearing people. The Gospel stories sound a little different once you realize that Jesus' warnings against the Pharisees in his day may fit your church members rather well!

Bible dictionaries vary in size and depth. A single-volume dictionary is a good buy for the beginning Bible student. Later you may want to get a multivolume set.

As you do some reading about key terms, be sure to jot down any learnings you want to remember.

Clarify the Literary Context

Here you need to answer two questions: "What biblical material immediately *precedes* the passage you are studying? What biblical material immediately *follows* the passage?" As a general rule, the longer the passage, the more material before and after you will want to read. If your focus is on a few verses, read at least the surrounding chapter. If your focus is on a whole chapter, read at least the chapter before and the chapter after.

Make a note of what is going on in the surrounding context. Suppose, for instance, that you have focused on 1 Corinthians 11:27. This verse is misunderstood by some people to mean that they must be morally and spiritually perfect if they are to partake of Holy Communion. And so they forego what is meant to be a means of grace. But a careful look at the surrounding verses (17-34) reveals that Paul was addressing a situation in which some were making gluttons and drunkards of themselves while others went hungry. His point was that all who partake of the Lord's meal should take care to share the food and drink. He wanted the Corinthian Christians to recognize that the Lord's Supper should be celebrated with a sense of unity and mutual care. It concerns living as the Body of Christ as much as it concerns eating a meal.

Take as another example the thirteenth chapter of that same letter to the Corinthians. Because of the sheer eloquence of the language, this chapter is frequently lifted out of its context and plopped down in a wedding ceremony or on a greeting card. But suppose you want to take a serious look at what God is saying here through the Apostle Paul. Look at chapter twelve; Paul is talking about gifts of the Holy Spirit and the Christian community as the Body of Christ. Now look at chapter fourteen; Paul is still talking about gifts of the Holy Spirit. Chapter 13 appears in the middle. What does that context imply? At the very least, it reminds us that love—the kind of love that Paul is talking about—is a *gift* from God, not a human achievement. And the context suggests that this gift of love is what somehow *enables* Christians to behave appropriately as members of the Body of Christ. Apart from the gift of love we neither use the other spiritual gifts properly nor live in a healthy community of believers.

Clarify the Canonical Context

The *canon* refers to the books officially recognized as part of the Bible. Asking about the canonical context means asking where the particular passage being studied is located in the Bible as a whole. What connections does this passage have to other places in the Bible? The more familiar you are with the sweep of the entire Bible, of course, the easier this step becomes. For instance, if you know something about the original Exodus from Egypt, you are more likely to appreciate what it meant for the Babylonian exiles 750 years later to be a part of a new Exodus, initiated by God, back to the land of Palestine. Or to take another example, if you remember the account of the Tower of Babel, you are likely to recognize the reversal in the story of Pentecost. In one case, languages were multiplied and confusion reigned. In the other case, a variety of languages became the occasion for a wondrous common understanding of God's power and purpose.

But a couple of Bible study tools can help even beginners make connections between the passage under study and the rest of the Bible. First, check the cross references in the Bible itself. Often the connecting passage illumines or is illumined by the passage you are studying. For instance, the cross-reference for Luke 3:4-6 will direct you to the source of the Old Testament quotation: Isaiah 40:3-5. And if you look up the cross-references for Jesus' words on the cross in the Gospel of Matthew chapter 27, verse 46, you will find that Jesus was quoting from the opening of Psalm 22. Another example: the meaning of Jesus' Last Supper with his disciples, recorded in Luke 22 is deepened if you recognize the linkage to the Old Testament Passover—and the cross-reference will point you to Exodus 12.

Another basic tool for Bible study that you can use to locate your passage in the wider biblical message is a *concordance*. Many people use a concordance only when they want to look up a half-remembered verse that keeps nagging their memory. But a concordance has a systematic place in Bible study too. Suppose you want to study a theme such as *redemption* (because it cropped up in a passage you were reading). A concordance will tell you where to find redemption in other passages in the Bible.

Clarify the Historical and Geographical Context

Our understanding of any important document is enhanced by knowing something about the situation in which it was written. Take Martin Luther King Jr.'s famous "Letter from a Birmingham Jail". We have a better grasp of that message if we know something about the man who wrote it, when he wrote it, what was going on in Birmingham and where Birmingham is located, the history of the Civil Rights Movement and so on.

Similarly, our understanding of a Bible passage is enhanced by answering questions such as: "Who wrote this? When? Where? What was going on at the time?" Suppose that you are reading a passage from the Book of Jeremiah. You need to know that Jeremiah was a prophet whose career spanned forty years (about 626-586 B.C.), and that the empire of Babylonia was about to crush Jeremiah's people of Judah and haul them away as captives. You need to know that, though his contemporaries dismissed him as a doomsayer and traitor, history proved Jeremiah right.

You can find this sort of background information in lots of places. But three types of study tools are easy to use and affordable. Bible *handbooks* help keep you from losing sight of the forest while in the trees. They typically present a thumbnail sketch of the content and historical context of each book of the Bible. (Most versions also include essays on all sorts of background material on various subjects from ancient measures, weights, money, and calendars to ancient manuscripts to archaeology.) General *introductions* to the Old Testament or New Testament weave more history into the explanations about the content and development of the Scriptures than is found in Bible handbooks. But the usefulness is similar: to get a sense of the big picture within which a particular passage is located. Another resource that can help is an *atlas* or *mapbook* of Bible lands. Even a quick look at a map can help you place a biblical passage in a geographic location and therefore make better sense of it.

State the Original Meaning of the Passage

For most of us, writing something down is helpful because it forces us to pull our thoughts together for review. So, take some time to digest everything you have learned about the passage you are studying. Then set down on paper what you think was the intended meaning of the passage for its original readers or listeners. Try not to jump ahead and apply the passage to *your* situation. First, be sure you have a clear sense of the meaning in the *ancient* situation.

What Does the Passage Mean Today?

Finally, you are ready for the "payoff" of in-depth Bible study. You want to figure out what the passage means for Christian readers today. *After* you have wrestled with the passage to clarify its original meaning, you need to ask yourself: "How is the world I live in (the big world and your little corner of it) like the world described in the Bible? What are the bedrock similarities underneath the differences?" To

71

POCKET GUIDE TO THE BIBLE

answer that, you will need to answer some additional questions. "In what ways am I and the other people in my world similar to the original audience? Do we share some essential needs across the centuries? Are we prone to similar faults that need correcting? Do we face the same kind of anxieties about life and death and human worth? Are we facing social problems similar to what ancient Israel and the early Christian church faced? Do we carry similar responsibilities for the moral health of families and communities?" Once you identify some ways in which contemporary people and situations are similar to the people and situations in the Bible passage, you will recognize that the Bible passage addresses *you* as well as its ancient audience.

Let's look at a few examples. Take Genesis 1-2. How is the world you and others live in like the world described in the Bible? What needs, problems, and issues do you face that are spoken to in this text? For one thing, we face an environmental crisis. To recover the true meaning of having *dominion* (as distinct from *domination*) would be no small gift today. Likewise, the report that Adam was placed in the garden to till and keep it carries implications for the way we treat the natural world. And the story of man and woman who are fit as *helper* and *partner* speaks to our age's confusion about the roles and worth of men and women.

Read Amos 5:10-15, 21-24. It sounds like a litany of contemporary social problems: a breakdown of the judicial system, exploitation of the poor, bribery of public officials. The prophet Amos contended that God is concerned about social justice, that religious piety cannot make up for indifference to the well being of the *whole* community. What does that imply for the behavior of Christians today?

Look at one of Jesus' parables from Matthew 20:1-16. Who are today's equivalent of the workers who toiled all day? Who are today's equivalent of those who worked just one hour? The tough—but absolutely essential—part of Bible study is to be ruthlessly honest about who you identify with in the Bible passage. Most middle-class people in Christian churches are offended by this story because they identify with the workers who toiled all day. We, like those workers, demand fairness and so find God's gracious goodness a bitter pill to swallow. So we find this parable a challenge to rethink the way we interpret reality and our place in it.

Finally look at 1 Corinthians 8. The issue surrounded eating meat, sold in the marketplace, which was left over from pagan sacrifices. Hardly the sort of thing that comes up in most congregations today! But think: do we face modern equivalents of eating meat offered to idols, things not wrong in themselves but a cause of a brother or sister falling? Then Paul's counsel to the Corinthians addresses us, too.

Gleaning the message that a Bible passage holds for us today *is* risky. But you can minimize that risk by repeatedly asking: "Is the message I see in this passage really compatible with the original message?" It's one thing to extend the message of a text to address modern parallels. But it's quite another to dismiss or violate the original intent of a passage. Beyond that check, we can only trust Paul's advice to the Christians at Philippi: "work out your own salvation with fear and trembling; for God is at work in you, both to will and to work for his good pleasure" (Philippians 2:12-13).

A Short Plan for Studying Bible Passages

This summary list of guidelines will help you study particular Bible passages in some depth. Feel free to copy these guidelines and use them as worksheets for your study. Then you can keep your study notes in a three-ring binder, providing you with both a record of your emerging skill as a Bible interpreter and a personal library of insights gleaned from the Bible.

1. What is the Bible passage you want to examine?
2. Read the passage carefully, word-for-word. Jot down any words or phrases that catch your eye as potential keys to what the passage is saying. Make a note of terms that are new to you.
3. Look up the key terms in a theological wordbook or a dictionary of the Bible. Keep a record of what you find.
4. Clarify the literary context of the passage. What biblical material immediately precedes and follows the passage you are studying?

5. Clarify the canonical context. Where is this passage located in the Bible as a whole? What connections does the passage have to other parts of the Bible?

6. Clarify the historical and geographical context. What was going on at the time the passage was written? Write what you find out about the author, date of writing, place of origin or destination, historical events, issues, and problems.

7. State the original meaning of the passage. Clarity and accuracy here are crucial to the success of the final step.

8. Explain what the passage means for Christian readers today. How is our situation like that of the persons who first heard the biblical passage? What needs, hopes, and fears do we share in common across the centuries that allow us to appropriate the ancient Word for our lives? What are the issues we face (or should face) that are equivalent to the issues faced in the Bible passages?